Figurative Language
and Other Literary Devices

Using Literature to Teach Literary Techniques

Metaphor

Oxymoron

Personification

Simile

Imagery

Hyperbole

Idiom

Irony

...and more!

Written by Rebecca Stark

Illustrated by Karen Birchak

ISBN-10: 1-56644-187-0
ISBN-13: 978-1-56644-187-2

© 2006 Educational Impressions, Inc., Hawthorne, NJ

Printed in the U.S.A.

TABLE OF CONTENTS

Figurative Language & Other Literary Devices

Figurative Language & Other Literary Devices

TO THE TEACHER

Literary techniques are the constructions of language used by an author to convey meaning. These techniques make the story more interesting to the reader. It is crucial that students learn to identify and understand these constructions. Familiarity with these techniques will prepare them not only for standardized tests, but also for their future education. The understanding of these devices will help students get more enjoyment from the fiction they read—both in and out of the classroom situation. This comprehensive unit uses examples from classic and modern literature to introduce and reinforce these techniques.

LITERARY DEVICES

The following literary terms / techniques are covered in this text:

- Connotation
- Dialogue
- Dialect
- Imagery
- Idiom
- Simile
- Metaphor
- Allusion
- Personification
- Hyperbole
- Understatement
- Irony
- Sarcasm
- Oxymoron
- Paradox
- Symbol
- Pun
- Alliteration
- Onomatopoeia

FORMAT

Each term is defined. One or more examples are given from classic and/or modern literature. Students are then given opportunities to identify, explain, and use the technique.

OBJECTIVES

Figurative Language & Other Literary Devices is designed to teach students in grades 5 through 8 literary terms and techniques to help them understand and analyze works of fiction.

At the end of this unit, students will be able to…

- identify the style of a work of literature;
- understand denotation and connotation;
- identify and understand dialogue;
- identify and understand dialect;
- identify and understand imagery;
- identify and understand idioms;
- identify and understand similes and metaphors;
- identify and understand allusion;
- identify and understand personification;
- identify and understand hyperbole;
- identify and understand understatement;
- identify and understand irony;
- identify and understand sarcasm;
- identify and understand oxymora;
- identify and understand paradox;
- identify and understand symbolism;
- identify and understand puns and other plays on words;
- identify and understand onomatopoeia, alliteration, and other forms of poetic language;
- use all of the above to help them analyze works of literature; and
- use figurative language and other literary techniques in their own writing.

Literary Devices

Literary Devices of Style

We refer to the way an author uses language as the **style** of a story. That style can be formal or informal. One of the most important factors is word choice. An author may choose to use simple, direct vocabulary or he or she may choose to use more elaborate or unusual vocabulary. Also, words with similar dictionary meanings, or denotations, often have different connotations. They evoke different feelings and thoughts. Other factors that affect style are dialogue, dialect, and idioms.

In addition to word choice, authors use a variety of literary techniques to create a story and to make that story more interesting. Imagery is the most commonly used literary technique. It appeals to the reader's senses—sight, sound, smell, touch, and taste—to help the reader form a mental picture of what is happening in the story.

Many authors use some form of figurative language. Figurative language is not meant to be taken literally. It encourages readers to use their imagination and to look at the world in new ways. Among the most common forms of figurative language are simile, metaphor, and personification. Other forms include pun, hyperbole, understatement, irony, oxymoron, and paradox. Authors also use poetic devices that rely on sound, such as alliteration and onomatopoeia, to add interest.

© Educational Impressions, Inc.

Common Literary Devices

The following literary devices of style are explained in this worktext:

- Connotation
- Dialogue
- Dialect
- Imagery
- Idiom
- Simile
- Metaphor
- Allusion
- Personification
- Hyperbole
- Understatement
- Irony
- Sarcasm
- Oxymoron
- Paradox
- Symbolism
- Pun
- Alliteration
- Onomatopoeia

Each term is defined. One or more examples are given from classic and/or modern literature. You will then be given opportunities to identify, explain, and use these techniques.

Figurative Language & Other Literary Devices

Connotation

It is important to understand denotation and connotation when reading a work of literature. **Denotation** is the clearly expressed meaning of a word or phrase. **Connotation** is the associated meaning of a word or phrase.

EXAMPLE FROM LITERATURE
Anne of Greene Gables, by L.M. Montgomery (Chapter 1: "Mrs. Rachel Lynde Is Surprised")

The author uses the word *meek* to describe Thomas Lynde: "Thomas Lynde, a meek little man whom Avonlea people called "Rachel Lynde's husband." The word *meek* means "showing patience and humility." However, the word has a negative connotation. The connotation is that he is submissive and that people, especially his wife, easily impose upon him.

CONNOTATION CATEGORIES
Label each word in the set as favorable, unfavorable, or neutral. Use the letters F, U, and N. You may have the same label for different words in the same set. Be aware that what has a positive connotation for you may have a negative one for someone else and vice versa!

1. house
   home
   mansion
   hovel

2. slender
   thin
   skinny
   emaciated

3. chef
   cook
   short-order cook

4. antique
   old
   out-dated

5. thrifty
   cheap
   frugal
   miserly

6. bargain
   haggle
   negotiate

7. smile
   smirk
   grin

8. confident
   proud
   conceited

Dialogue

Dialogue, the spoken words between the characters, is often used by an author to bring the story to life. It can tell us how a character thinks or feels. It can also take the place of exposition; in other words, it can tell us what is happening or what has happened. Because people usually speak in a more informal manner than the way in which they write, a conversational style is usually more informal than one that does not include dialogue.

Dialogue can add to a story in several ways. Sometimes it helps the reader determine the setting of a story. It can inform the reader about an event that has occurred in the past. It can also help the reader predict an event that may occur in the future. Often we learn a lot about the characters from the words they speak and from the way others speak to them. Dialogue can do a lot to arouse our interest and spark our curiosity!

EXAMPLE FROM LITERATURE
The Hound of the Baskervilles, by Sir Arthur Conan Doyle

The following example is from *The Hound of the Baskervilles,* by Sir Arthur Conan Doyle. In Chapter 2, "The Curse of the Baskervilles," Dr. Mortimer explains to Sherlock Holmes the reason for his visit.

" 'This family paper was committed to my care by Sir Charles Baskerville, whose sudden and tragic death some three months ago created so much excitement in Devonshire…' "

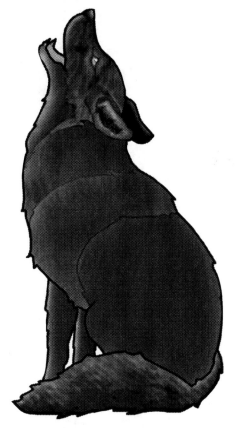

Dr. Mortimer goes on to explain the circumstances of the death and what he had observed near the scene: " 'Mr. Holmes, they were the footprints of a gigantic hound!' "

These passages not only pique our interest, but also give us information about an important event which has occurred—the death of Charles Baskerville.

Figurative Language & Other Literary Devices

Uses of Dialogue

Dialog can serve many purposes.

- It may help develop the setting.

- It may explain an event that has already occurred.

- It may predict an event that may (or may not) occur.

- It may provide insight into one or more characters.

- It may be used to arouse interest.

- It may be used to create suspense.

What's the Purpose?

Anne of Green Gables, written by L.M. Montgomery, is filled with interesting dialogue. Read each example. Then describe the purpose or purposes the dialogue serves. You may use the chart on the previous page to help you.

1. The following dialogue is from Chapter 1, "Mrs. Rachel Lynde Is Surprised." Mrs. Rachel Lynde is questioning Marilla Cuthbert about her brother Matthew.

" 'We're all pretty well,' said Mrs. Rachel. 'I was kind of afraid *you* weren't though, when I saw Matthew starting off today. I thought maybe he was going to the doctor's.'

'Oh, no, I'm quite well although I had a bad headache yesterday,' she said. 'Matthew went to Bright River. We're getting a little boy from the orphan asylum in Nova Scotia and he's coming on the train tonight.' "

_____

_____

_____

_____

_____

_____

_____

2. As the conversation proceeds, Mrs. Rachel reacts to what Marilla has told her.

" 'Well, Marilla, I'll just tell you plain that I think you're doing a mighty foolish thing....' "

_____

_____

_____

_____

_____

_____

_____

Figurative Language & Other Literary Devices

Creating Dialogue

Choose one of the following situations. Create a dialogue that might be used in a story based upon that situation. Your dialogue should provide relevant information about the plot, one or more of the characters, the setting, or another aspect of the story.

SITUATION #1

A woman has just learned that her state lottery ticket contains all of the winning numbers. The prize is $5,000,000 and she is the sole winner! Her husband, who does not even know that she has purchased a ticket, has just arrived home.

SITUATION #2

You have taken second place in a statewide essay competition. Your best friend has won first prize. The prizes, which are $100 and $1,000 respectively, are to be awarded next week. You have accidentally come across proof that your friend bought his essay from an internet source. Your friend sees that you are upset and asks you what is wrong.

_____ : _____

_____

_____

_____ : _____

_____

_____

_____ : _____

_____

_____

_____ : _____

_____

_____

Figurative Language & Other Literary Devices   © Educational Impressions, Inc.

Dialect

Sometimes an author incorporates the use of dialect when creating dialogue. **Dialect** is speech that reflects the vocabulary, speech patterns, and grammar of a particular geographic region or of a particular social or economic group. The use of dialect can help create the tone of the book. It can also be helpful in making the setting apparent and in characterization.

EXAMPLES FROM LITERATURE
The Adventures of Tom Sawyer, by Mark Twain

Mark Twain used dialect in his popular novel *The Adventures of Tom Sawyer.* The dialect he used is typical of the lower class living in the Mississippi Valley in the mid- to late-1800s.

Mark Twain

In Chapter 1, Aunt Polly says, " 'Hang the boy, can't I ever learn anything? Ain't he played me tricks enough like that for me to be looking out for him by this time?' "

Later in that chapter she tries to get Tom to admit that he played hooky. She says, " 'Tom, it was middling warm in school, warn't it?' "

Treasure Island, by Robert Louis Stevenson

In *Treasure Island,* Robert Louis Stevenson used dialect typical of an 18th-century seaman.

In Chapter 1 Black Dog comes to Jim's father's inn and says, " 'This is a handy cove, and a pleasant sittyated grog-shop. Much company, mate?' "

Robert Louis Stevenson

In Chapter 8 Long John Silver questions Tom Morgan and asks, " 'Come, no, what was he jawing—v'yages, cap'ns, ships? Pipe up! What was it?'
'We was a-talkin' of keel-hauling,' answered Morgan."

Figurative Language & Other Literary Devices

Interpreting Dialect

These excerpts from well-known works of literature contain dialect. Rewrite them using standard English.

1. From *A Long Way From Chicago,* by Richard Peck ("The Mouse in the Milk")
Situation: Grandma is holding a shotgun on the two brothers who had come to steal the gun.

" 'Skin to the church and get there maw and paw,' Grandma said briefly to me."

_____

_____

_____

2. From *The Outsiders,* by S.E. Hinton (Chapter 1)
Situation: Soda is telling Ponyboy that his brother Darry really cares a lot about him.

" 'Listen kiddo, when Darry hollers at you…he don't mean nothin'…Don't take him serious…you dig, Pony? Don't let him bug you. He's really proud of you 'cause you're so brainy…Savvy?' "

_____

_____

_____

_____

_____

3. From *Tuck Everlasting,* by Natalie Babbitt (Chapter 16)
Situation: The man in the yellow suit has told the constable that he knows where to find Winnie.

" 'How come *you're* so deep in it?' asked the constable suspiciously. 'Maybe you're in cahoots with the kidnappers.…You should have reported it right off, when you saw her get snatched.' "

_____

_____

_____

_____

Interpreting Dialect, Continued

4. From *Roll of Thunder, Hear My Cry,* by Mildred D. Taylor (Chapter 4)
Situation: T.J. is explaining why Mr. Tatum was tarred and feathered. Mr. Barnett is the owner of the mercantile.

" Mr. Tatum's s'pose to done told him that he ain't ordered up all them things Mr. Barnett done charged him for. Mr. Barnett said he had all them things Mr. Tatum ordered writ down and when Mr. Tatum asked to see that list of his, Mr. Barnett says, 'You callin' me a liar, boy?' and Mr. Tatum says, 'Yessuh, I guess I is!' That done it!"

_____

_____

_____

_____

_____

_____

_____

5. From *Treasure Island,* by Robert Louis Stevenson (Chapter 28: "In the Enemy's Camp")
Situation: John Hawkins has been captured by Long John Silver.

" 'The short and the long of the whole story is about here: you can't go back to your own lot, for they won't have you; and without you start a third ship's company all by yourself, which might be lonely, you'll have to jine with Cap'n Silver.' "

_____

_____

_____

_____

_____

_____

Figurative Language & Other Literary Devices

Imagery

Authors use **imagery** to appeal to their readers' senses. Imagery can add to a work of fiction in several ways. It may help the author create a mood or evoke emotions. Sometimes it helps to reinforce the characterization the author is trying to develop. Imagery can also be used to develop a theme.

EXAMPLE FROM LITERATURE:
Mrs. Frisby and the Rats of NIMH, by Robert C. O'Brien

In the final chapter the author uses imagery to set the mood.

"The sun had set. They went…and lay down on the soft moss….The brook swam quietly and the warm wind blew through the newly opened leaves….They went to sleep."

SIGHT
sun had set
newly opened leaves

TOUCH
soft moss
warm wind

SOUND
swam quietly

Figurative Language & Other Literary Devices   © Educational Impressions, Inc.

Imagery in *The Call of the Wild*

Jack London made excellent use of imagery in his novel *The Call of the Wild.* Think about the mental pictures created by the phrases in bold. Then fill in the chart on the following page.

1. From Chapter I: "Into the Primitive"

"Buck lived at a **big house** in the **sun-kissed Santa Clara Valley....**It stood...half hidden among the trees, through which glimpses could be caught of the **wide, cool veranda** that ran around its four sides. The house was approached by **gravelled driveways** which wound about through **wide-spreading lawns** and under the **interlacing boughs of tall poplars....**There were...rows of **vine-clad servants' cottages,** an endless and **orderly array of outhouses, long grape arbors, green pastures, orchards, and berry patches.** Then there was the pumping plant for the artesian well, and the big cement tank where Judge Miller's boys took their morning plunge and **kept cool** in the **hot afternoon."**

2. From Chapter I: "Into the Primitive"

"For two days and nights this express car was dragged along at the tail of **shrieking locomotives;** and for two days and nights Buck neither ate nor drank. In his anger he had met the first advances of the express messengers with **growls,** and they had retaliated by teasing him. When he flung himself against the bars, **quivering and frothing,** they laughed at him and taunted him. They **growled and barked** like detestable dogs, **mewed,** and flapped their arms and **crowed....**He did not mind the hunger so much, but the lack of water caused him severe suffering and fanned his wrath to fever-pitch....The ill treatment had flung him into a fever, which was fed by the inflammation of his **parched and swollen throat and tongue."**

3. From Chapter II: "The Law of Club and Fang"

"A **whiff of warm air** ascended to his nostrils, and there, curled up under the snow in a snug ball, lay Billy."

4. From Chapter V: The Toll of Trace and Trail

"It was beautiful spring weather, but neither dogs nor humans were aware of it....The whole long day was a **blaze of sunshine.** The **ghostly winter silence** had given way to the **great spring murmur** of awakening life. This **murmur arose** from all the land, fraught with the joy of living....The **sap was rising** in the pines. The **willows and aspens were bursting out** in young buds. **Shrubs and vines were putting on fresh garbs of green. Crickets sang** in the nights, and in the days all manner of creeping, crawling **things rustled** forth into the sun. **Partridges and woodpeckers were booming and knocking** in the forest. **Squirrels were chattering, birds singing,** and overhead **honked the wild-fowl** driving up from the south in cunning wedges that split the air."

Figurative Language & Other Literary Devices

Chart the Images

For each bold phrase in the previous activity, think about the sense to which sense the author is appealing. Then fill in the chart. A phrase may be placed in more than one category.

PHRASES THAT APPEAL TO SENSE OF SIGHT

PHRASES THAT APPEAL TO SENSE OF SOUND

PHRASES THAT APPEAL TO SENSE OF TOUCH

PHRASES THAT APPEAL TO SENSE OF SMELL OR TASTE

Figurative Language & Other Literary Devices

Create a Mental Picture

Choose one of the following experiences and write a descriptive paragraph about it. Use images that appeal to as many of the five senses as you can.

A Day at the Amusement Park

A Walk in the Woods

An Afternoon at the Movies

Collecting Seashells at the Beach

A Trip to the Zoo

Waiting to Board an Airplane

_____

_____

_____

_____

_____

_____

_____

_____

_____

_____

_____

_____

_____

Figurative Language & Other Literary Devices

Figurative Language

Figurative language is the use of language in a way that differs from the original, intended meaning of the word or words. In other words, the words should not be taken literally. Sometimes we refer to the various forms of figurative language as "figures of speech."

COMMON FORMS OF FIGURATIVE LANGUAGE

Idiom

Simile

Allusion

Metaphor

Personification

Hyperbole

Understatement

Oxymoron

Paradox

Symbol

Pun

Verbal Irony

Idioms

An **idiom** is a figure of speech that does not make sense if you take each individual element literally. For example, suppose someone said, "It's raining cats and dogs." Most people would understand that it is raining heavily; they would not expect to see animals falling from the sky!

Some idioms, like the one above, become so common that they lose their effectiveness; we call overused figures of speech **clichés**. It's best not to use clichés too often in your writing, especially if you can think of a more original way to express your idea.

EXAMPLES FROM LITERATURE
Anne of Green Gables, by L.M. Montgomery

The following examples are from *Anne of Green Gables,* by L.M. Montgomery.

1. The following excerpt is from the chapter entitled "Morning at Green Gables."

" 'For pity's sake hold your tongue,' said Marilla. 'You talk entirely too much for a little girl.' "

"Hold your tongue" is an idiom. In this sentence, it means "be quiet." Marilla did not want Anne to actually take hold of her tongue!

2. The following excerpt is from the chapter entitled "Anne's Bringing-up Is Begun."

" 'When I went to live with Mrs. Hammond it just broke my heart to leave Katie Maurice. She felt dreadfully, too,' said Marilla."

"Broke my heart" is an idiom. In this sentence, it means "made me extremely sad." Anne's heart did not actually break!

3. The following excerpt is from the chapter entitled "Anne to the Rescue."

" '[Geometry] is casting a cloud over my whole life. I'm such a dunce at it, Matthew.' "

"Casting a cloud over" is an idiom. In this sentence, it means "making her life gloomy." She does not look up and see a huge cloud over her head wherever she goes!

Figurative Language & Other Literary Devices

Working with Idioms

For each excerpt, replace the portion in bold with standard English.

1. From *Treasure Island,* by Robert Louis Stevenson (Chapter 28,"In the Enemy's Camp")
Situation: Long John Silver is speaking to the captured Jim Hawkins.

" **'I'll give you a piece of my mind.** I've always liked you, I have, for a lad of spirit and the picter of my own self when I was young and handsine.' "

I'll Have to tell you something.

2. From *Little Women,* by Louisa May Alcott (Chapter 21, "Laurie Makes Mischief, and Jo Makes Peace")
Situation: Teddy, also known as Laurie, has apologized for a prank.

" **'I keep turning over new leaves,** and spoiling them, as I used to spoil my copy-books, and I make so many beginnings there never will be an end.' "

3. From *Little Women,* by Louisa May Alcott (Chapter 36, "Beth's Secret")
Situation: Beth has confided the severity of her illness to Jo. This is Jo's response.

" 'It shall be stopped, **your tide must not turn so soon.'** "

4. From *Little Women,* by Louisa May Alcott (Chapter 43, "Surprises")
Situation: Jo has asked where Amy is, and Teddy has answered by referring to Amy as his wife. Jo reacts.

" 'What can you expect, when **you take one's breath away,** creeping in like a burglar, and **letting cats out of bags** like that?' "

Figurative Language & Other Literary Devices

Some Common Idioms

to cross that bridge

bread and butter

to let the cat out of the bag

to put one's foot down

to catch one's eye

out of the blue

to be at the end of one's rope

to pull one's leg

to be tongue tied

to lend a hand

to draw the line

to be on thin ice

to pull strings

to bury the hatchet

to be all thumbs

a fly in the ointment

to have cold feet

to have a green thumb

a dime a dozen

to bite one's tongue

a wolf in sheep's clothing

to be easy as pie

to burn one's bridges

icing on the cake

to turn over a new leaf

to have a chip on one's shoulder

a taste of one's own medicine

to lose one's head

to be in the doghouse

to lend an ear

to bite the hand that feeds one

to be a third wheel

to let sleeping dogs lie

to be on the house

to keep am eye on someone

to rock the boat

Add five common idioms to the list.

_____

_____

_____

_____

_____

Figurative Language & Other Literary Devices

Guess the Idiom

Try to figure out the missing idiom. Choose from the list on the previous page. Change pronouns, verb forms, etc., as necessary.

1. From *Bud, Not Buddy,* by Christopher Paul Curtis (Chapter 13)
Situation: Steady Eddy, the sax man, has asked Bud to put the case with his saxophone in the trunk of the car.

" 'And be careful, that's my _____ in there. ' "

_____

2. From *Maniac Magee,* by Jerry Spinelli (Chapter 2)
Situation: Maniac Magee surprises people he doesn't know by greeting them.

"They stopped. They…wondered: Do I know that kid? Because people just didn't say that to strangers, _____."

_____

3. From *The Wind in the Willows,* by Kenneth Graham (Chapter 1,"The River Bank")
Situation: Mole was sitting on the grass, looking across the river.

"A dark hole in the bank opposite, just above the water's edge _____
and dreamily he fell to considering what a nice snug dwelling-place it would make."

_____

4. From *A Day No Pigs Would Die,* by Robert Newton Peck (Chapter 4)
Situation: Mr. Tanner has given Robert a pig of his own.

"I was going to bring her into the kitchen, but Mama _____ on that idea."

_____

Guess the Idiom, Continued

5. From *A Year Down Yonder,* by Richard Peck ("Away in a Manger")

Situation: Mary Alice and the other girls in her home-economics class were making hot pads to give as Christmas presents.

"Ina-Rae was my crocheting partner, and she was _____ with a crochet hook. Her hot pad bunched up…like a skullcap."

_____

6. From *The High King,* by Lloyd Alexander (Chapter XIII, "Darkness")
Situation: Doli advises his friends to march with him to the cavern and to follow the main shaft in order to catch up with the Cauldron-Born.

" 'We'll stop them one way or another. How, I don't know. That doesn't matter for the moment. We'll _____.' "

_____

Follow-up Activity: Clichés
Choose three idioms from the list. Write two sentences for each. One using the common idiom, or cliché. The other using a more creative figure of speech.

_____

_____

_____

_____

_____

_____

_____

_____

_____

Figurative Language & Other Literary Devices

You Don't Mean That!

Choose three idioms. Write two definitions: one that gives the literal meaning of the words and one that shows the idiomatic meaning of the expression. Write a sentence for each meaning.

IDIOM: _____

Literal Meaning: _____

Sentence: _____

_____

Idiomatic Meaning: _____

Sentence: _____

_____

IDIOM: _____

Literal Meaning: _____

Sentence: _____

_____

Idiomatic Meaning: _____

Sentence: _____

_____

IDIOM: _____

Literal Meaning: _____

Sentence: _____

_____

Idiomatic Meaning: _____

Sentence: _____

_____

Metaphors and Similes

Both metaphors and similes are figures of speech that compare two unlike things. A **simile** makes the comparison clearly, usually by using the words *like* or *as*. A **metaphor** does not use *like* or *as* to make the comparison. In other words, a simile says something is *like* something else. A metaphor says something *is* something else.

EXAMPLES FROM LITERATURE
Little Women, by Louisa May Alcott

Louisa May Alcott used many similes and metaphors in her classic novel *Little Women.*

SIMILES
This excerpt from Chapter 16 describes how Jo feels after selling her hair. It includes a simile which compares Jo to a shorn sheep.

"Away went Jo, feeling like a shorn sheep on a wintry day."

This excerpt from Chapter 20 describes how Jo and Meg feel when Beth finally comes out of her delirium and seems to be out of danger. The simile compares Meg and Jo to storm-beaten boats that are finally back and safe in the harbor.

"With a blissful sense of burdens lifted off, Meg and Jo closed their weary eyes, and lay at rest, like storm-beaten boats, safe at anchor in a quiet harbor."

METAPHOR
In Chapter 7 Jo realizes that Amy has used an incorrect allusion to describe their friend Laurie; therefore, she compares Amy to a goose. It is a metaphor because in this sentence Amy is said to *be* a goose and not just *like* a goose.

" 'That little goose means a centaur, and she called him a cyclops,' exclaimed Jo."

Figurative Language & Other Literary Devices

Unlikely Comparisons

Each of the following excerpts contains a simile or a metaphor. For each figure of speech in bold whether tell whether it is a simile or a metaphor and which two things are being compared. Then give the reason for the comparison.

1. From *The Lost World,* by Arthur Conan Doyle (Chapter 10, "The Most Wonderful Things Have Happened")

Situation: The male pterodactyls, who are perched on stones high above, are being described.

"Their huge, membranous wings were closed by folding their forearms, so that they sat **like gigantic old women,** wrapped in hideous web-coloured shawls."

This is a _____.

_____

_____

_____

2. From *The Secret Garden,* by Frances Hodgson Burnett (Chapter 1, "There Is No One Left")

Situation: Mary's mother had not wanted a little girl, so she put her in the care of an Ayah.

"Because the Mem Sahib would be angry if she was disturbed by her crying, by the time she was six years old she was as **tyrannical and selfish a little pig** as ever lived."

This is a _____.

_____

_____

_____

3. From *Criss Cross,* by Lynn Rae Perkins (Chapter 4, "Radio Show")

Situation: Debbie had been sunbathing, but she did not turn over.

"In their fronts-only sunburned state, her bare legs **reminded** Hector **of a freshly opened, unscooped box of Neapolitan ice cream,** minus the chocolate stripe."

This is a _____.

_____

_____

_____

Unlikely Comparisons, Continued

4. From *Catherine, Called Birdy,* by Karen Cushman ("24TH OF SEPTEMBER")

Situation: Catherine is upset because her father seeks to arrange a marriage for her with a wealthy, but boring man.

"Now **my father, the toad,** conspires to sell me **like a cheese** to some lack-wit seeking a wife."

This is a _____.

_____ and _____ are compared

because _____

_____

This is a _____.

_____ and _____ are compared

because _____

_____

5. From *James and the Giant Peach,* by Roald Dahl (Chapter 2)

Situation: James has been sent to live with his two horrible aunts, one of whom is described here.

"Aunt Spongy was enormously fat and very short. She had…one of those white flabby faces that looked as though it had been boiled. She was **like a great white soggy overboiled cabbage."**

This is a _____.

_____ and _____ are compared

because _____

_____

6. From *Kira, Kira,* by Cynthia Kadohata (Chapter 2)

Situation: Katie tells how her father described her mother.

"My mother **was a delicate, rare, and beautiful flower.…**She was so delicate that if you bumped in to her accidentally, you would bruise her."

This is a _____.

_____ and _____ are compared

because _____

_____

Figurative Language & Other Literary Devices

Creative Comparisons

Part 1: Write a sentence describing each situation using a simile.

1. Sue is wearing a black-and-white sweater her grandmother knit for her.

2. Jack hadn't eaten all day. He is at a buffet and has loaded his plate with food.

3. It is a beautiful day. You are in a restaurant overlooking the river watching the sailboats.

4. You are in a crowded elevator that has stalled.

_____

_____

_____

_____

_____

_____

_____

Part 2: Rewrite each sentence replacing the words in bold with a metaphor.

1. I gazed at the **blue sky** above.

2. As I sipped my lemonade, I stared at the **expansive, beautiful green lawn.**

3. Jenny had been in the pool for hours. "Would my little **girl** like to come out for a while and have a snack?" her mother asked.

4. The child's mother exclaimed, "Look at my little **boy.** He just loves to climb trees!"

_____

_____

_____

_____

_____

_____

_____

Allusion

Allusion is similar in some ways to metaphors and similes. **Allusion** is a reference to something outside the work in which it is found. For example, an author might describe a difficult task by writing, "It was a Herculean task."

EXAMPLE FROM LITERATURE:
Little Women, by Louisa May Alcott
Louisa May Alcott used allusion in Chapter 7 of *Little Women* in a humorous way.

In the first excerpt Amy uses an incorrect allusion when she sees their friend Laurie ride by them on horseback.

" 'That boy is a perfect cyclops, isn't he?' said Amy one day, as Laurie clattered by on horseback, with a flourish of his whip as he passed."

At first Jo is offended by Amy's allusion and she expresses her anger. " 'How dare you say so, when he's got both his eyes?' "

Amy responds by defending herself: " 'I didn't say anything about his eyes, and I don't see why you need fire up when I admire his riding.' "

When Jo realizes that Amy has alluded to the wrong mythological creature, she exclaims, " 'That little goose means a centaur, and she called him a cyclops.' "

Figurative Language & Other Literary Devices

It's an Allusion

Identify and explain the allusion in each excerpt.

1. From *Bud, Not Buddy,* by Christopher Paul Curtis (Chapter 3)
Situation: The excerpt describes the way Bud battled the bat in the shed.
"I raised the rake over my head again, closed my eyes and swung it like I was Paul Bunyon chopping down a tree with one blow."

_____

_____

_____

_____

2. From *Hoot,* by Carl Hiaasen (Chapter 20)
Situation: Chuck reacted when Beatrice rushed over to Ray and took his hand.
" 'Aw, that's real cute. Just like Romeo and Juliet,' Chuck Muckle taunted."

_____

_____

_____

_____

3. From *Johnny Tremain,* by Esther Forbes (Chapter V: "The Boston Observer")
Situation: Rab came to the rescue of the Webb twins, who were being tormented by the butcher's son. He fought off not only the butcher's son, but also the butcher, his wife, and another son.
"It was strange that a boy who could fight like that…never quarreled, never fought, and he had almost nothing to say about this really Homeric battle."

_____

_____

_____

_____

Allusions as Context Clues

For each, use the allusion to help you choose the correct word or phrase to complete the sentence.

1. I was in awe of my brother Jack's achievements; he was a real Thomas Edison.

   Jack was an _____.

            a. artist   b. inventor   c. author

2. I remarked that Jeanine's new boyfriend was quite an Adonis.

   He was very _____.

            a. handsome   b. smart   c. wealthy

3. Zachary told his sister that she was being a Pollyanna.

   Her sister was a(n) _____.

            a. realist   b. pessimist   c. optimist

4. Upon entering the room, Sam felt as if he had entered the Twilight Zone.

   Things seemed _____ to Sam.

            a. strange   b. joyful   c. boring

5. "We should call an expert," said Jake. "This situation calls for Sherlock Holmes."

   They need a _____.

            a. bodyguard   b. detective   c. tutor

6. Her Achilles' heel was her love of chocolate.

   Her love of chocolate was her _____.

            a. weak point   b. strong point   c. trademark

Figurative Language & Other Literary Devices

A Biographical Sketch

Write a paragraph describing someone. The person may or may not be famous. Your sketch may even be autobiographical! Use an allusion in your opening sentence. Your details should support that allusion.

You may allude to one of the following people or characters, or you may choose one of your own.

Possible Suggestions for Your Allusion

Shirley Temple

Superman

Wonder Woman

Dr. Seuss

Picasso

Darth Vader

Sir Galahad

Mona Lisa

Peter Pan

Rip Van Winkle

_____

_____

_____

_____

_____

_____

_____

_____

_____

_____

_____

_____

Personification

Personification is the giving of human qualities to inanimate objects, ideas, or animals. These qualities include thoughts, feelings, and actions.

EXAMPLES FROM LITERATURE:

Out of the Dust, by Karen Hesse

Out of the Dust contains excellent examples of personification. Set in Oklahoma in the 1930s, the book is in the form of a young girl's journal. It gives readers great insight into what it was like to live during the terrible dust storms of that time period. The personification (indicated in bold) of the wheat, the snow, the land, and especially the rain in these excerpts makes their importance even more apparent.

"The winter wheat…**stood helpless.**" (March 1934)

"Snow…**soothed** the **parched lips** of the land." (May 1935)

"It was the **kindest** kind of rain that fell." (May 1935)

"[The rain] kept coming…**dancing** from the heavens." (May 1935)

The Secret Garden, by Francis Hodgson Burnett (Chapter 21)

In the following excerpt the blue sky is given the human quality of looking down.

"It was like a king's canopy, a fairy king's.…Between the blossoming branches of the canopy bits of blue sky **looked down.**"

Around the World in Eighty Days, by Jules Verne (Chapter 14)

In the following excerpt the sea is given the human ability to plan to delay Phileas Fogg.

"Phileas Fogg gazed at the tempestuous sea, which seemed to be **struggling** especially **to delay him.**"

Figurative Language & Other Literary Devices

How Humanlike!

For each excerpt tell what is being personified and how it is personified. Be sure to include the word or words that are most important to the personification in your explanation.

1. From *Little Women,* by Louisa May Alcott (Chapter 12)

"When the sun peeped into the girls' room early next morning to promise them a fine day, he saw a comical sight."

_____

_____

2. From *The Secret Garden,* by Frances Hodgson Burnett (Chapter 4)

"But the flower-beds were bare and wintry and the fountain was not playing."

_____

_____

3. From *Oliver Twist,* by Charles Dickens (Chapter 38)

"There are smiling fields and waving trees in England's richest county."

_____

_____

4. From *The Time Machine,* by H.G. Wells (Chapter 4)

"Above me towered the sphinx....It seemed to smile in mocking of my dismay."

_____

_____

5. From *Amos Fortune, Free Man,* by Elizabeth Yates (1781–1789)

" '[The mountain] Monadnock says it will be good weather today,' Amos would announce."

_____

_____

How Human-like! Continued

6. From *A Single Shard,* by Linda Sue Park (Chapter 5)

"The plum trees took on their gold and scarlet autumn garb."

_____

_____

7. From *Missing May,* by Cynthia Rylant (Chapter 9)

"The green-and-white road signs kept teasing us along with mentions of Capitol Street."

_____

_____

8. From *The Westing Game,* by Ellen Raskin (Chapter 4, "The Corpse Found")

"At last slow morning crept up the cliff."

_____

_____

9. From *The House of Dies Drear,* by Virginia Hamilton (Chapter 3)

"[The house] seemed to crouch on the side of a hill."

_____

_____

10. From *Treasure Island,* by Robert Louis Stevenson (Chapter 17)

"The ebb tide, which had so cruelly delayed us, was now making reparation, and delaying our assailants."

_____

_____

Figurative Language & Other Literary Devices

Personification Sentences

Write a sentence for each in which you give the object or idea human qualities. You may make the nouns plural if you wish.

1. a flower (or specific flower): _____

_____

2. a tree (or specific tree): _____

_____

3. the sun: _____

_____

4. the moon: _____

_____

5. a pillow: _____

_____

6. a raindrop: _____

_____

7. a leaf: _____

_____

8. a rocket ship: _____

_____

9. thunder: _____

_____

10. lightning: _____

_____

Anthropomorphism

Anthropomorphism, which is sometimes confused with personification, is when animals or inanimate objects are portrayed as people. It is not the same as personification. For example, in *Mrs. Frisby and the Rats of Nimh,* written by Robert C. O'Brien, most of the characters are mice or rats. This is an example of anthropomorphism; it is not personification.

For each, tell whether the excerpt is an example of personification or anthropomorphism.

1. From *The Jungle Book,* by Rudyard Kipling (Mowglie's Brothers)

" 'Augrh!' said Father Wolf, 'it is time to hunt again.' "

This excerpt is an example of _____.

2. From *The Wind in the Willows,* by Kenneth Grahame (Chapter 1, "The River Bank")

"The Mole had been working hard all the morning, spring cleaning his little home. First with brooms, then with dusters...."

This excerpt is an example of _____.

3. From *Where the Red Fern Grows,* by Wilson Rawls (Chapter XVII)

"With its loud roaring, the north wind seemed to be laughing at us."

This excerpt is an example of _____.

4. From *The Tale of Despereaux,* by Kate Di Camillo (Chapter Nine, "The Right Question")

"The Mouse Council sent Furlough to collect Despereaux."

This excerpt is an example of _____.

5. From *The Midwife's Apprentice,* by Karen Cushman (Chapter 8, "The Turns")

" First they cooked parsnips with sugar and spices and yeast and poured this into casks, where the fermenting mixture sang loud and sweet as it turned into wine."

This excerpt is an example of _____.

Figurative Language & Other Literary Devices

Hyperbole

Hyperbole is a deliberate exaggeration. Hyperbole can be used to create a mood, to emphasize a fact, or to add humor.

Examples of Hyperbole

I'm so hungry, I could eat a horse.

There were a million people at the party.

I think I just gained fifty pounds after eating this huge dinner.

I must have a million mosquito bites.

It will take a year to clean this closet!

EXAMPLES FROM LITERATURE:

Anne of Green Gables by L.M. Montgomery
In the chapter entitled "Anne's Apology," Anne must apologize for her rude behavior—behavior she does not truly regret. She uses hyperbole in her apology.

"I could never express all my sorrow, no not if I used up a whole dictionary....I deserve to be punished and cast out by respectable people for ever."

The Call of the Wild, by Jack London (Chapter 5)
In this chapter the woman named Mercedes has been told that she, her husband, and her brother must eliminate half their load if they expect to reach Dawson. Jack London used hyperbole to describe the way she lessened the load.

"And in her zeal, when she had finished with her own, she attacked the belongings of her men and went through them like a tornado."

Don't Exaggerate!

Underline the hyperbole in each excerpt. Rewrite the underlined portion without using hyperbole.

1. From *The Secret Garden,* by Frances Hodgson Burnett (Chapter 20, "I Shall Live Forever—and Ever—and Ever!")
Situation: Mary wants to know what Colin is thinking about.
" 'What big eyes you've got, Colin,' she said. 'When you are thinking they get as big as saucers.' "

_____

_____

2. From *The Witch of Blackbird Pond,* by Katherine Paterson (Chapter 8)
Situation: The chores were overwhelming to Kit.
"A shearing had brought a veritable mountain of gray wool to be washed and bleached and dyed."

_____

_____

3. From *A Connecticut Yankee in King Arthur's Court,* by Mark Twain (Chapter 12)
Situation: Hank Morgan, a Connecticut Yankee who finds himself in King Arthur's court, is wearing a suit of armor in the heat. The heat was making him itch.
"Well, you know, when you perspire that way, in rivers, there comes a time when you…itch."

_____

_____

4. From *To Kill a Mockingbird,* by Harper Lee (Chapter 11)
Situation: Mrs. Dubose insulted Atticus, causing Jem to lose his temper and destroy her bushes. Usually Jem and his sister Scout went to meet their father as he came home from work, but after this incident they did not. The following is from Scout's point of view.
"Two geological ages later, we heard the soles of Atticus's shoes scrape the front steps."

_____

_____

Figurative Language & Other Literary Devices

Davy Crockett

Hyperbole is an integral part of tall tales. Although Davy Crockett was a real person, we remember him almost as much for his tall tales as for his heroic deeds.

For each "fact" about Davy Crockett, decide whether or not hyperbole is being used. Circle "truth" or "exaggeration" as appropriate.

1. Davy Crockett was born in Tennessee in 1766.

   TRUTH / EXAGGERATION

2. At three years old, Davy wrestled and killed a large bear by squeezing the bear until it fell.

   TRUTH / EXAGGERATION

3. Davy was given a rifle as a young boy and named it Old Betsy.

   TRUTH / EXAGGERATION

4. He became a very good shot.

   TRUTH / EXAGGERATION

5. He became such a good shot that the animals learned of his reputation. As soon as they saw him, they surrendered.

   TRUTH / EXAGGERATION

6. He was elected to the Tennessee legislature in 1823.

   TRUTH / EXAGGERATION

7. He was elected to the U.S. Congress in 1827 and 1829, but he was defeated in 1831.

   TRUTH / EXAGGERATION

8. Once it was so cold that people's words froze in midair. You had to pluck their words down out of the air and fry them to know what was said.

   TRUTH / EXAGGERATION

9. He joined the Texas Volunteers in their fight to hold the Alamo.

   TRUTH / EXAGGERATION

10. Davy Crockett died at the Alamo on March 6, 1836.

    TRUTH / EXAGGERATION

Creating Hyperbole

We all use hyperbole from time to time. Write a sentence for each situation using hyperbole, or overstatement.

1. Situation: You are very hungry.

_____

_____

2. Situation: You are waiting for your friend, who is very late.

_____

_____

3. Situation: You are watching a boring TV show.

_____

_____

4. Situation: You are very tired.

_____

_____

5. Situation: It is a very hot day.

_____

_____

6. Situation: It is a very cold day.

_____

_____

7. Situation: You see a very tall building.

_____

_____

Figurative Language & Other Literary Devices

Understatement

Understatement is the opposite of hyperbole. Like hyperbole, understatement can be either serious or funny.

EXAMPLES FROM LITERATURE:

Robinson Crusoe, by Daniel DeFoe
Early in *Robinson Crusoe,* in the chapter entitled "The Storm," Robinson Crusoe's companion asks him after a strong storm if he was frightened by the "capful of wind."

This understatement has the effect of trivializing the main character's belief that it was a terrible storm.

Charlie and the Chocolate Factory, by Roald Dahl
In Chapter 17 Augustus Gloop ignored Mr. Wonka's warnings and fell into the chocolate river. He has been sucked into a glass pipe. The others are watching the chocolate swishing around him when he suddenly disappears.

" 'Call the fire brigade!' yelled Mrs. Gloop.
'Keep calm!' cried Mr. Wonka.…'Augustus has gone on a little journey, that's all.' "

Explain the understatement in the above excerpt.

_____

_____

_____

_____

_____

Creating Understatement

Write a sentence or two to refer to each subject using understatement.

1. An Erupting Volcano

_____

_____

2. An Enormous, Expensive Yacht

_____

_____

3. A Huge Mansion

_____

_____

4. A Category-5 Hurricane

_____

_____

5. Mount Everest

_____

_____

6. A Cruise Around the World

_____

_____

7. A Blizzard

_____

_____

Figurative Language & Other Literary Devices

Litote: A Kind of Understatement

A **litote** is a special kind of understatement. It uses a negative statement to state a positive idea.

EXAMPLES OF LITOTE

To describe a good artist, you might say, "He's not a bad artist."

To describe a driver who has had many accidents, you might say, "He's not the greatest driver."

EXAMPLES FROM LITERATURE:

Birches, by Robert Frost
At the end of his poem, the poet states, "One could do worse than be a swinger of birches."
The inference is that it would be good to be a swinger of birches.

The View from Saturday, by E.L. Konigsburg
The following excerpt is from the section called "Julian Narrates When Ginger Played Annie's Sandy." Nadia's dog, Ginger, had been chosen for a part in a school play. Michael Froelich's dog, Arnold, was to be the understudy. Nadia did not trust Michael.

"During the actual performances [Michael] and Arnold were to stay backstage and out of sight—unless something happened to Ginger. Did leaving Arnold as understudy make Froelich feel like an underdog?"
"I was not without worry."

Identify and explain the litote in the above excerpt.

_____

_____

Create an original scenario. Use a litote to explain the situation.

_____

_____

_____

_____

_____

Irony

There are four types of irony: verbal, dramatic, situational, and cosmic. **Verbal irony** is a figure of speech in which the speaker says the opposite of what he or she means. In **dramatic irony** the reader (or audience) knows more than the character knows; the reader knows that what the character believes or says is not so. **Situational irony** involves improbable, unexpected, sometimes unfair occurrences. When fate is involved—especially if the result is tragic—it is called **cosmic irony**, or irony of fate.

EXAMPLES FROM LITERATURE:

Verbal Irony
Julius Caesar, by William Shakespeare
In verbal irony, what is said contradicts what is meant. An example of verbal irony is found in Act III, Scene 2 of *Julius Caesar,* by William Shakespeare. In his famous speech that begins, "Friends, Romans, countrymen, lend me your ears," Mark Antony uses verbal irony:

> Friends, Romans, countrymen, lend me your ears;
> I come to bury Caesar, not to praise him.
> . . . .
> The noble Brutus
> Hath told you Caesar was ambitious:
> If it were so, it was a grievous fault,
> And grievously hath Caesar answer'd it.
> Here, under leave of Brutus and the rest—
> For Brutus is an honourable man;

Mark Antony says, "Brutus is an honourable man." The reader (or audience) knows that Antony does not really think that Brutus is honorable. (This is repeated several times in the rest of the speech.)

"A Modest Proposal," by Jonathan Swift
The narrator's preposterous proposal in this satirical essay, written by Swift in 1729, exemplifies the importance of making sure readers recognize the irony! The narrator suggests that the Irish poor sell their children as food as a solution to their problems, which were caused by poverty and discrimination.

© Educational Impressions, Inc. *Figurative Language & Other Literary Devices*

Dramatic Irony
Romeo and Juliet, by William Shakespeare

Romeo and Juliet, by William Shakespeare, contains many instances of irony. An example of dramatic irony is found in Act IV, Scene 2. The irony is that the reader (or audience) knows that the clothing referred to in this excerpt will be used for her funeral and not her wedding. Because the reader knows but the character speaking does not, we call it dramatic irony.

> Nurse, will you go with me into my closet,
> To help me sort such needful ornaments
> As you think fit to furnish me to-morrow?

Situational Irony
The Necklace, by Guy de Maupassant

The Necklace, by Guy de Maupassant, is an excellent example of situational irony. Mme. Loisel borrows a necklace from a wealthy friend and loses it. Her husband buys a replacement necklace for 36,000 francs, which Mme. Loisel gives to her friend without mentioning the loss. The Loisels live in poverty the next ten years in order to pay for the necklace. They do not see the friend during that time. One day Mme. Loisel sees her friend. Readers and Mme. Loisel are both surprised to learn that the original necklace is not valuable.

" 'Oh!—My poor Mathilde, how you are changed.'
'Yes, I have had hard days since I saw you, and many troubles,—and that because of you.'
'Of me?—How so?'
'You remember that diamond necklace that you lent me to go to the ball at the Ministry?'
'Yes. And then?'
'Well, I lost it.'
'How can that be?—since you brought it back to me?'
'I brought you back another just like it. And now for ten years we have been paying for it. You will understand that it was not easy for us, who had nothing. At last, it is done, and I am mighty glad.'
Mme. Forester had guessed.
'You say that you bought a diamond necklace to replace mine?'
'Yes. You did not notice it, even, did you? They were exactly alike?'
And she smiled with proud and naive joy.
Mme. Forester, much moved, took her by both hands:—
'Oh, my poor Mathilde. But mine were false. At most they were worth five hundred francs!' "

Ironic Situations

Label each of these situations as verbal irony, dramatic irony, situational irony, or cosmic irony.

1. A hard-working woman with a modest income has bought lottery tickets twice a week for about ten years and never won more than ten dollars. One night she checks online and realizes that she is the sole winner of five million dollars. That night her house burns down with the ticket in it.

_____

2. A teenage girl has broken her leg in a skiing accident and is lying in a hospital bed. Her friend enters and asks her how she is doing. "I'm having a great day," she replies.

_____

3. Romeo thinks Juliet has died but readers know that she is not really dead.

_____

4. Amy arrives at Jamie's house soaking wet from the storm. Jamie says to Amy, "Great weather, isn't it?"

_____

5. Jake stayed up all night studying for his exam. He knew everything perfectly. He fell asleep about five minutes into the test.

_____

Create ironic situations:

Verbal Irony:

Dramatic Irony:

Situational or Cosmic Irony:

Figurative Language & Other Literary Devices

Sarcasm

Sarcasm is a form of verbal irony. It is a cutting remark and may involve saying the opposite of what is meant. Originally, the term applied only to remarks meant to make the victim the object of ridicule. Today, however, it is also used to refer to kind remarks.

EXAMPLE FROM LITERATURE:

The Lost World, by Arthur Conan Doyle (Chapter 11)
Lord John asks Professor Challenger his opinion about the mark on the iguanodon's hide. Lord John had asked him to be quiet; therefore, the professor replies sarcastically.

" 'If your lordship will graciously permit me to open my mouth, I shall be happy to express my sentiments.' "

Identify and Explain
Explain the sarcasm in each of the following excerpts.

1. From *Crispin, the Cross of Lead,* by Avi (Chapter 16)
Situation: Crispin has been giving short, evasive answers.
Bear says, " 'You have a gifted way of speech.' "

_____

_____

2. From *A Year Down Yonder,* by Richard Peck ("Rich Chicago Girl")
Situation: Mildred has been harassing Mary Alice, so Grandma asks Mildred if her father is still in the penitentiary. Mildred says that he was framed. The excerpt is Grandma's response.
" 'Oh, I guess them sheep off the Bowman farm found their own way into your pen.' "

_____

_____

3. From *The View from Saturday,* by E.L. Konigsburg ("Nadia Tells of Turtle Love")
Situation: Nadia's parents are divorced and it is her father's time to be with her. Nadia is annoyed because her father keeps looking at his watch. He explains that he has an appointment in an hour. Nadia responds, " 'I am sure it is an important appointment.' "

_____

_____

Oxymora

An **oxymoron** is a phrase made up of seemingly contradictory or incongruous terms. Originally, the term was used to describe only the deliberate juxtaposition of contradictory terms for effect, such as "deafening silence." Today it is commonly used to describe terms that are based on alternate meanings of a word or words, such as "jumbo shrimp."

Examples of Oxymora

act naturally

active retirement

almost exactly

anxious patient

boneless rib

burning cold

cautiously optimistic

deafening silence

definite maybe

icy hot

jumbo shrimp

larger half

old news

only choice

organized chaos

original copy

small crowd

sweet sorrow

tough love

unbiased opinion

virtual reality

working vacation

EXAMPLE FROM LITERATURE:

Romeo and Juliet, by William Shakespeare
William Shakespeare used an oxymoron in his very famous passage from Act 2, Scene 2 of *Romeo and Juliet* when Juliet says good night.
"Good night, good night! Parting is such sweet sorrow."

"Sweet sorrow" is an oxymoron.

Figurative Language & Other Literary Devices

Working with Oxymora

Identify and explain the oxymoron in each of the following excerpts.

1. From *A Day No Pigs Would Die,* by Robert Newton Peck (Chapter 3)
Situation: Robert's father explains why he and Mr. Tanner keep up a fence to mark the boundaries of their properties. Robert compares it to being at war with each other and thinks it is strange because they are friends.
Mr. Newton says, " 'It's a peaceable war. If I know Benjamin Franklin Tanner, he'd fret more than me if his cows found my corn.' "

_____

_____

_____

2. From *Crispin, The Cross of Lead,* by Avi (Chapter 26)
Situation: Bear is trying to teach Crispin to play the recorder and shouts at him in his frustration. At first Crispin is afraid, but then he realizes that Bear would not carry out his threats.
"As the day wore on I realized he was mostly bluster.…While I didn't doubt he could have done the ghastly acts…it was but a rough kindness."

_____

_____

_____

3. From *Frankenstein,* by Mary Shelley (Volume I, Chapter VI)
Situation: Victor's father is explaining why he hadn't written until his return. Victor's young brother had been killed and his father didn't want to tell him until his return.
"I was at first tempted to write only a few lines, merely mentioning the day at which I should expect you. But that would be a cruel kindness, and I dare not do it. What would be your surprise, my son, when you expected a happy and gay welcome, to behold, on the contrary, tears and wretchedness?"

_____

_____

_____

Create three original sentences using oxymora. You may choose from the list on the previous page, or you may create your own.

Paradox

A **paradox** is similar to an oxymoron. It is a statement or situation that seems contradictory. Closer study, however, reveals a truth.

EXAMPLES FROM LITERATURE

"Nothing Gold Can Stay," by Robert Frost

Nothing Gold Can Stay

Nature's first green is gold,
Her hardest here to hold.
Her early leaf's a flower;
But only so an hour.
Then leaf subsides to leaf.
So Eden sank to grief,
So dawn goes down to day.
Nothing gold can stay.

—*Robert Frost*

The poem starts out with two paradoxes. "Green is gold" seems to be contradictory; however, in New England the first signs of spring, represented by the word "green," are the goldish leaves of the willow and birch trees. "Leaf's a flower" also seems to be contradictory; however, the early leaves are flower-like in appearance.

A Tale of Two Cities, by Charles Dickens

In the famous opening lines of *A Tale of Two Cities,* Charles Dickens used paradoxes to describe the period in which the story was set.

"It was the best of times, it was the worst of times, it was the age of wisdom, it was the age of foolishness, it was the epoch of belief, it was the epoch of incredulity, it was the season of Light, it was the season of Darkness, it was the spring of hope, it was the winter of despair, we had everything before us, we had nothing before us, we were all going direct to Heaven, we were all going direct the other way."

Romeo and Juliet

The Prologue in the first act sets the play in Verona, where two households are feuding. These families are the Montagues and the Capulets. Romeo is a Montague, and Juliet is a Capulet. The author tells us in the Prologue that the pair of ill-fated lovers—Romeo and Juliet—will kill themselves because of this ancient grudge the families hold against each other.

Romeo and Juliet contains many oxymora and paradoxes.

1. From Act I, Scene I (Romeo is speaking.)

Alas, that love, whose view is muffled still,
Should, without eyes, see pathways to his will!
Where shall we dine? O me! What fray was here?
Yet tell me not, for I have heard it all.
Here's much to do with hate, but more with love.
Why, then, O brawling love! O loving hate!
O any thing, of nothing first create!
O heavy lightness! serious vanity!
Mis-shapen chaos of well-seeming forms!
Feather of lead, bright smoke, cold fire, sick health!
Still-waking sleep, that is not what it is!
This love feel I, that feel no love in this.
Dost thou not laugh?

Underline the oxymora and circle the paradoxes in the above passage.

2. From Act I, Scene V (Juliet is speaking.)

My only love sprung from my only hate!
Too early seen unknown, and known too late!
Prodigious birth of love it is to me,
That I must love a loathed enemy.

Explain the paradoxes in the first and last lines of the above excerpt.

_____

_____

_____

_____

_____

Figurative Language & Other Literary Devices   © Educational Impressions, Inc.

Symbols

Authors sometimes use **symbols** to express a theme. An object, person, or event stands for an abstract idea or feeling. That symbol will have not only its real, concrete meaning but also its symbolic meaning. Some symbols are universally recognized; examples are a heart for love, a skull for death, and a flag for patriotism. Other symbols are contextual; in other words, they are constructed for a particular work.

EXAMPLE FROM LITERATURE:

To Kill a Mockingbird, by Harper Lee
In *To Kill a Mockingbird,* the mockingbird is a symbol of innocence. In the novel it symbolizes harmless, gentle people, such as Tom and Boo, who are often destroyed by the cruel, insensitive behavior of others.

In Chapter 10 Atticus advised, " 'Shoot all the bluejays you want…but remember it's a sin to kill a mockingbird.' " Miss Maudie concurred and said, " 'Mockingbirds don't do one thing but make music for us to enjoy.' "

In Chapter 25 Mr. Underwood wrote an editorial in which "he likened Tom's death to the senseless slaughter of songbirds by hunters and children."

In Chapter 30, Mr. Tate noted that it would be a sin to make Boo go through the ordeal of a trial. Scout pointed out that "it'd be sort of like shootin' a mockingbird."

Figurative Language & Other Literary Devices

Thinking About Symbols

Read the excerpt or excerpts. Then answer the question that follows.

1. From *Robinson Crusoe,* by Daniel Defoe ("A Footprint")
BACKGROUND INFORMATION: Robinson Crusoe has been stranded on a deserted island. He has been alone for many years and has seen no hint that another human being could be on the island. After all these years, he is shocked to see a footprint in the sand.

"It happened one day about noon going toward my boat, I was exceedingly surprised with the print of a man's naked foot on the shore, which was very plain to be seen in the sand.
. . . .
To have seen one of my own species would have seemed to me a raising me from death to life, and the greatest blessing that Heaven itself, next to the supreme blessing of salvation, could bestow; I say, that I should now tremble at the very apprehensions of seeing a man, and was ready to sink into the ground at but the shadow or silent appearance of a man's having set his foot in the island."

What do you think the footprint symbolizes?

_____

_____

_____

2. From *Across Five Aprils,* by Irene Hunt (Chapters 1 and 5)
BACKGROUND INFORMATION: Set during the American Civil War, this novel is about a border-state family. Jethro is nine years old when the story begins in April 1861. He has become a field worker and, therefore, is allowed to eat at the first table with his parents and older brothers.

"Coffee was an adult luxury....On this day of the boy's graduation to 'first table' honors...Bill took a dried crust of bread...and after soaking it...placed it on his brother's plate." (Chapter 1)

"It was fifteen miles to Newton; to cover that distance with a team, to do the chores and handle money—that was a man's job....They loaded the wagon the next morning....Ellen [Jethro's mother] made him share her coffee that morning." (Chapter 5)

What do you think the coffee symbolizes?

_____

_____

_____

Which Symbol?

Suppose you were writing a novel. Think of a symbol you might use throughout your novel to represent each of the following concepts.

1. Importance of Family   _____

2. Love   _____

3. Happiness   _____

4. Passage of Time   _____

5. Life Cycles   _____

6. Good   _____

7. Evil   _____

8. Peace   _____

9. Maturing   _____

10. Innocence   _____

Symbols can represent different ideas in different stories. Choose one of the following. Think of at least two different concepts it might represent in a story. Include one or two sentences to explain the symbolism.

> Rolls Royce
> Little Red Wagon
> Band of Gold
> Book

_____

_____

_____

_____

_____

_____

Figurative Language & Other Literary Devices

Puns

A **pun** is a play on words. Most puns are based upon different meanings of the same word or on different words with similar pronunciations. Puns are usually, but not always, humorous.

EXAMPLE FROM LITERATURE:

Charlie and the Chocolate Factory, by Roald Dahl (Chapter 18)
"A poached egg isn't a poached egg unless it's been stolen from the woods in the dead of night."

The pun is based upon the two meanings of the word *poach.* *Poach* can mean "to cook in hot liquid." It can also mean "to steal from another's property."

Identify and Explain

Identify and explain the pun in each of the following excerpts.

1. From *A Connecticut Yankee in King Arthur's Court,* by Mark Twain (Chapter 2)
Situation: The "Connecticut Yankee" has come across a slim, young boy. The boy explains that he is a page in the king's court.
"This was an airy slim boy in shrimp-colored tights that made him look like a forked carrot....
He...informed me that he was a page."
" 'Go 'long,' I said. 'You ain't more than a paragraph.' "

_____

_____

_____

2. From *Missing May,* by Cynthia Rylant (Chapter 7)
Situation: Aunt May has died and Summer, Uncle Ob, and Summer's classmate Cletus are going to see a spiritualist to try to contact Aunt May's spirit. During their travels Cletus remarks that he would like to be a Renaissance Man.
"Ob laughed and slapped Cletus on the knee. 'After our little trip, you might be calling yourself a Rent-a-Seance Man!' "

_____

_____

_____

_____

Devices of Sound: Alliteration

Some literary devices rely on sound. **Alliteration** is one such device. It is the repetition of initial consonant sounds. Alliteration not only adds a poetic sound, it also helps emphasize the phrases.

EXAMPLE FROM LITERATURE:

The Westing Game, by Ellen Raskin
The author uses many alliterative phrases. Some examples are "prattling pretender," "sequined spectacles," "somber silence," and "dastardly deed."

Alliteration Search
Find the alliteration in the following excerpts and circle the alliterative words.

From *The Great Gilly Hopkins,* by Katherine Paterson ("Sarsaparilla to Sorcery")
Situation: Gilly is imagining what it would be like if her mother came and got her.
"I'd turn from gruesome Gilly into gorgeous, gracious, good, glorious Galadriel. And grateful—I'd be so grateful!"

From "The Raven," by Edgar Allan Poe
Situation: A man is mourning the loss of his deceased lover. This is the first stanza of the poem, which was published in 1845.

> Once upon a midnight dreary, while I pondered weak and weary,
> Over many a quaint and curious volume of forgotten lore,
> While I nodded, nearly napping, suddenly there came a tapping,
> As of some one gently rapping, rapping at my chamber door.
> " 'Tis some visitor," I muttered, "tapping at my chamber door—
> Only this, and nothing more."

Create Alliteration Sentences
Use alliteration in one or two sentences about yourself.

_____

_____

_____

_____

_____

Figurative Language & Other Literary Devices

Devices of Sound: Onomatopoeia

Onomatopoeia is the use of a word that mimics the sound it represents. Some examples are *buzz, jingle, moan, meow, quack, moo, bang, click,* and *roar.* Onomatopoeia is often used in poetry.

EXAMPLE FROM LITERATURE:

"The Bells," by Edgar Allan Poe (1849)
Read the following excerpts to see how Poe used onomatopoeia and repetition to take us from the merriment of the tinkling and jingling of the bells in the first stanza to their melancholy groaning and moaning in the fourth.

I
Hear the sledges with the bells—
Silver bells!
What a world of merriment their melody
    foretells!
How they tinkle, tinkle, tinkle,

. . . .
From the jingling and the tinkling of the bells.

II
Hear the mellow wedding bells,
Golden bells!
What a world of happiness their harmony
    foretells!

. . . .
To the rhyming and the chiming of the bells!

III
Hear the loud alarum bells—
Brazen bells!
What a tale of terror, now, their turbulency tells!

. . . .
How they clang, and clash, and roar!
What a horror they outpour.

. . . .
By the twanging,
And the clanging,

. . . .
In the clamor and the clangor of the bells!

IV
Hear the tolling of the bells—
Iron Bells!
What a world of solemn thought their monody
    compels!

. . . .

For every sound that floats
From the rust within their throats
Is a groan.

. . . .

And who, tolling, tolling, tolling,
In that muffled monotone,

. . . .
To the moaning and the groaning of the bells.

Circle the onomatopoetic words in the above excerpts.

Identifying Onomatopoeia

Look for onomatopoeia in the following excerpts. Write the onomatopoetic words.

1. From *James and the Giant Peach,* by Roald Dahl (Chapter 27)
Situation: The Cloud-Men were hurling hailstones at James and his companions.
"The hailstones came whizzing through the air like bullets from a machine gun."

_____

_____

2. From *The Pied Piper of Hamelin,* by Robert Browning (Verse VII, lines 106-110)
Situation: This excerpt describes the piper's playing.

    And ere three shrill notes the pipe puttered,

    You heard as if an army muttered;

    The muttering grew to a grumbling;

    And the grumbling grew to mighty rumbling;

    And out of the house the rats came tumbling.

_____

_____

3. From *The Tale of Despereaux,* by Kate DiCamillo (Chapter 21, "The Queen's Last Words")
Situation: A rat had fallen into the queen's bowl of soup.
"In response, the queen flung her spoon in the air and made an incredible noise, a noise that was in no way worthy of a queen, a noise somewhere between the neigh of a horse and the squeal of a pig."

_____

_____

     Figurative Language & Other Literary Devices

Onomatopoetic Words

The following is a list of some onomatopoetic words.

bang	cuckoo	kerplunk	squeak
boom	drip	knock	squeal
buzz	gong	meow	squish
chime	groan	moan	swish
clang	growl	mumble	tinkle
clank	grunt	murmur	wail
clop	gurgle	mutter	whack
cluck	hiccup	sizzle	wheeze
crackle	hiss	slurp	whinny
crash	honk	sob	whiz
creak	howl	splash	yelp
crunch	hum	splat	zip

See how many you can add to the list!

Write three sentences using onomatopoetic words.

_____

_____

_____

_____

_____

_____

_____

Figurative Language & Other Literary Devices

Post-Unit Activities

Post-Unit Activities

Create five analogies. Each should include two or more literary terms.

Describe an embarrassing situation using hyperbole.

Draw pictures to illustrate three idioms. Have your classmates guess the idioms you are portraying.

Use understatement to describe something good you or someone else did.

Create a word search of literary devices.

Write a paragraph describing yourself. Use at least two similes and/or metaphors in your description.

Use allusion to describe someone you admire.

Tell a knock-knock joke that uses a pun.

Research the origin of the word *oxymoron.* Judge the use of that word to describe that particular figure of speech.

Two other devices of sound are assonance and consonance. Define the terms and give an example of each.

Use the song "You've Got to Be Carefully Taught," written by Rodgers and Hammerstein for the play *South Pacific,* to teach a lesson about verbal irony and why it is important to recognize an author's use of it.

Look for figurative language in your favorite book. Chart the figures of speech you find. Judge whether or not the figurative language added to your enjoyment of the book.

Define the terms "metonymy" and "synechdoche" and give an example of each.

Use litote to describe yourself.

Name the Technique

For each excerpt, identify the literary device in bold.

_____   1. From *Peter Pan,* by J.M. Barrie

"There is no **beating about the bush,** for we know quite well what it was, and have got to tell. It was Peter's cockiness."

_____   2. From *Catherine, Called Birdy,* by Karen Cushman

"We are at an inn tonight in a room with seven people and **seven thousand fleas.**"

_____   3. From *The High King,* by Lloyd Alexander

"Night turn to noon and rivers burn with **frozen fire** ere Dyrnwyn be regained."

_____   4. From *The Lost World,* by Arthur Conan Doyle

"There was a letter with…my name scrawled across the envelope in **a hand-writing which looked like barbed-wire railing.**"

_____   5. From *Holes,* by Louis Sachar

"A sign on the door said **WRECK ROOM.** Nearly everything in the room was broken."

_____   6. From *The Hound of the Baskervilles,* by Sir Arthur Conan Doyle

"Mr. Sherlock Holmes, who was usually very late in the mornings, **save upon those not infrequent occasions when he was up all night,** was seated at the breakfast table."

7. From *Peter Pan,* by J.M. Barrie

_____

"Everything was wrong. Nana, who had been barking distressfully all the evening, was quiet now. **It was her silence they had heard.**"

8. From *Tuck Everlasting,* by Natalie Babbitt

_____

"The road veered sharply…as if, for the first time, **it had reason to think where it was going,** and passed around."

9. From *Walk Two Moons,* by Sharon Creech

_____

"Two blocks from Margaret Cadaver's was the place where my father and I were now going to live.…Little birdhouses in a row—and **one of those birdhouses was ours.**"

10. From *The Outsiders,* by S.E. Hinton

_____

" 'The mist was what was pretty,' Johnny said. 'All gold and silver…Too bad it couldn't stay like that…'
'Nothing gold can stay.' I was remembering a poem I read once…Robert Frost wrote it!"

11. From *A Long Way from Chicago,* by Richard Peck

_____

"Grandma…wasn't the first person people ran to with news. **She wasn't what you'd call a popular woman.**"

12. From *The Sign of the Beaver,* by Elizabeth George Speare

_____

"In the silence, **Matt's heart beat so loudly they all surely must have heard it.**"

Figurative Language & Other Literary Devices

Crossword Puzzle

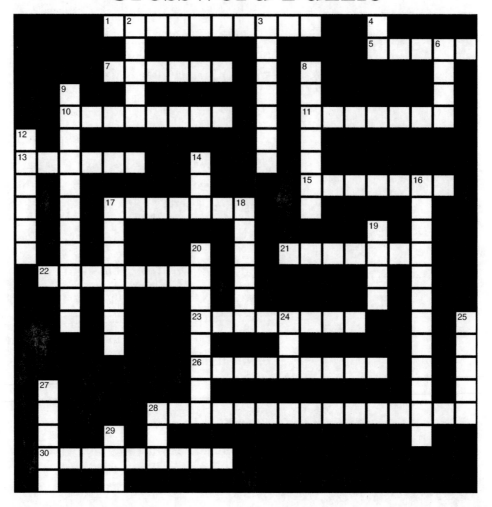

ACROSS

1. Language that should not be taken literally.
5. The way in which an author uses language.
7. A comparison of two unlike things using *like* or *as*.
10. A phrase made up of contradictory terms.
11. Similes and metaphors do this.
13. Author of *The Call of the Wild*.
15. A statement or situation that seems contradictory.
17. Author of *Oliver Twist*.
21. A cutting, ironic remark.
22. A conversation between two or more characters.
23. A reference to something outside the work in which it is found.
26. An exaggeration.
28. Giving human traits to inanimate objects and ideas.
30. Author of *Treasure Island*.

DOWN

2. A figure of speech that cannot be taken literally.
3. In alliteration these sounds are alike.
4. Word often used in a simile.
6. Word often used in a simile.
8. A passage taken from another work.
9. The associated meaning of a word or phrase.
12. Author of *Little Women*.
14. Author of "The Bells."
16. Use of a word that sounds like the sound it represents.
17. The use of language particular to a region and/or social class.
18. Object that stands for abstract idea.
19. Author of *Charlie and the Chocolate Factory*.
20. Comparison of two unlike things without the use of *like* or *as*.
24. Title bestowed upon Arthur Conan Doyle.
25. Author of *The Adventures of Tom Sawyer*.
27. Author of "Nothing Gold Can Stay."
28. A play on words.
29. Author of *Crispin, Cross of Lead*.

Appendix

Glossary of Literary Terms

Alliteration: The repetition of initial consonant sounds in two or more consecutive or neighboring words.

Allusion: A reference to something outside the work in which it is found.

Antagonist: The opponent of the main character, or protagonist.

Anthropomorphism: When animals or inanimate objects are portrayed as people.

Character: An imaginary person in a work of fiction.

Character development: The method used by an author to develop a character.

Character trait: A distinguishing characteristic, or quality, of a character.

Characterization: The method used by the author to give readers information about a character; a description or representation of a person's qualities or peculiarities.

Climax: The moment in a story when the action reaches its greatest conflict.

Conflict: The struggle within a character, between characters, between a character and society, or between a character and a force of nature.

Connotation: The associations that are suggested or implied by a word that go beyond its dictionary meaning.

Denotation: The dictionary meaning of a word.

Denouement: The part of the plot where the main dramatic conflict is worked out; the plot may or may not have a happy ending. (Also called resolution.)

Dialect: A variety of a language that is distinguished from the standard form by pronunciation, grammar, and/or vocabulary.

Dialogue (dialog): Conversation between two or more characters.

Exposition: The beginning of a work of fiction; the part in which readers are given important background information.

Falling action: The action that comes after the climax and before the resolution.

Figurative language: Description of one thing in terms usually used for something else. Simile and metaphor are examples of figurative language.

Flashback: Insertion of an earlier event into the normal chronological sequence of a narrative.

Foil: A character with traits opposite to those of the main character.

Foreshadowing: The use of clues to give readers a hint of events yet to occur.

Genre: A category of literature.

Historical fiction: Fiction represented in a setting true to the history of the time in which the story takes place.

Hyperbole: An exaggeration used for effect.

Idiom: An expression whose meaning cannot be determined by its literal expression.

Image: A mental picture.

Imagery: The use of language that appeals to the senses and produces mental images; the use of figures of speech or vivid descriptions to produce mental images.

Irony (situational): An outcome contrary to what was or might have been expected.

Irony (verbal): The use of words to express the opposite of their literal meaning.

Metaphor: A figure of speech that compares two unlike things without the use of *like* or *as*.

Mood: The feeling that the author creates for the reader.

Narrator: The voice and implied speaker who tells the story.

Onomatopoeia: The use of words that mimic the sounds they represent.

Oxymoron: A figure of speech made up of seemingly contradictory parts.

Paradox: A statement or situation that seems contradictory but reveals a truth.

Personification: The bestowing of human qualities on inanimate objects, ideas, or animals. (See the difference between personification and anthropomorphism.)

Plot: The ordered structure, or sequence, of causal events in a story.

Figurative Language & Other Literary Devices

Point of view: The perspective from which a story is told; the relation of the narrator to the story.

Protagonist: The main character.

Pun: A humorous play on words that are similar in sound but different in meaning.

Realistic fiction: True-to-life fiction; people, places, and happenings are similar to those in real life.

Resolution: The part of the plot where the main dramatic conflict is worked out; the plot may or may not have a happy ending. (Also called denouement.)

Rising action: Events in a plot that occur after the exposition but before the climax.

Sarcasm: A form of verbal irony in which a person says the opposite of what he or she means.

Satire: A literary work that pokes fun at individual or societal weaknesses.

Sequencing: The placement of story elements in a narrative order, usually chronological.

Setting: The time and place in which the main story events occur.

Simile: A figure of speech that clearly compares two unlike things through the use of *like* or *as.*

Stereotype: A character whose personality traits represent a group rather than an individual.

Style: The author's manner of writing, including grammatical structures, type of vocabulary, and the use of figurative language and other literary techniques.

Suspense: Quality that causes readers to wonder what will happen next; apprehension about what will happen.

Symbolism: The use of an object, character, or idea to represent something else.

Theme: The main idea of a literary work; the message the author wants to convey.

Tone: The attitude of the author towards his or her writing.

Understatement: To state something less strongly than the facts would indicate.

Connotation (Page 10) These answers reflect the opinion of the author. Students' answers may differ!

1. N, F, F, U
2. F, N, U, U
3. F, N, N
4. F, N, U
5. F, U, F, U
6. F, U, N
7. F, U, N
8. F, F, U

What's the Purpose? (Page 13)

1. The dialogue helps set the story in eastern Canada. It explains why Matthew left and where he was going. It predicts that another character will enter the story. It implies that Mrs. Rachel is curious.

2. This implies that Mrs. Rachel is not merely curious, but nosy. We now also know that she is very outspoken and that she gives her opinions freely.

Interpreting Dialect (Pages 16–17) Answers may vary.

1. "Rush to the church and ask their mother and father to come here," Grandma said abruptly.

2. "Listen, Ponyboy. When Darry shouts at you, he doesn't mean what he says. Don't take him seriously. Do you understand, Pony? Don't let it bother you. He's really proud of the fact that you're so smart. Do you understand?"

3. "Why do you know so much about it?" asked the constable suspiciously. "Maybe you conspired with the kidnappers. You should have reported it as soon as you saw them take her."

4. "Supposedly, Mr. Tatum told Mr. Barnett that he hadn't ordered all the things for which Mr. Barnett charged him. Mr. Barnett said that he had written down all the things that Mr. Tatum had ordered. When Mr. Tatum asked to see the list, Mr. Barnett asked if he was calling him a liar. Mr. Tatum replied that he was. That was what caused it [Mr. Tatum being tarred and feathered]."

5. "This is a summary of the situation: You can't go back to your old shipmates, because they don't want you. Unless you start a third ship's company alone, which might be lonely, you'll have to join with me."

Imagery: Chart the Images (Pages 19–20)

These phrases appeal to the sense of sight: big house, wide…veranda, gravelled driveways, widespreading lawns, interlacing boughs of tall poplars, vine-clad servants' cottages, orderly array…, quivering and frothing, sap was rising, willows and aspens were bursting out, and shrubs and vines were putting on fresh garbs of green.

These appeal to the sense of sound: shrieking locomotives, growls, growled and barked, mewed, crowed, ghostly winter silence, great spring murmur, murmur arose, crickets sang, things rustled, partridges and woodpeckers were booming and knocking, squirrels were chattering, birds singing, and honked the web-fowl.

These appeal to the sense of touch: sun-kissed Santa Clara Valley, cool verandas, kept cool, hot afternoon, parched and swollen throat and tongue, blaze of sunshine, and whiff of warm air.

This phrase appeals to the sense of smell: whiff of warm air.

Figurative Language & Other Literary Devices

Working with Idioms (Page 24)

1. I'll tell you what I think.
2. I keep starting over.
3. Things must not get worse for you so soon. (In other instances, it could mean "get better.")
4. What can you expect when you startle someone…and share surprising secrets like that?

Some Common Idioms (Page 25) Answers will vary, but the following are some possibilities.

to get off on the wrong foot   to be all bark and no bite   to be on the same page
to be a drop in the bucket   to have an ax to grind   to be on pins and needles
to be a piece of cake   to beat around the bush   to add fuel to the fire

Guess the Idiom (Pages 26–27)

1. bread and butter
2. out of the blue
3. caught his eye
4. put her foot down
5. all thumbs
6. cross that bridge when we come to it

Similes and Metaphors: Unlikely Comparisons (Pages 30–31)

1. Simile: The male pterodactyls are compared to old women because their wings resembled shawls.
2. Metaphor: Mary and a pig are compared because Mary is tyrannical and selfish.
3. Simile: Debbie's legs and Neapolitan ice cream are compared because of their stripes. (Note: In this simile the phrase "reminded of" takes the place of *like* or *as.)*
4. Metaphor: Catherine's father and a toad are compared because she doesn't think much of either.
Simile: Catherine is compared to cheese because her father wants to sell her as he would a piece of cheese.
5. Simile: Aunt Spongy and an overboiled cabbage are compared because Aunt Spongy had a flabby face.
6. Metaphor: Katie's mother and a rare flower are compared because she is rare, delicate and beautiful.

It's an Allusion (Page 34)

1. The allusion is to the legendary Paul Bunyon, known for his great strength. Bud's fear made him strong.
2. The allusion is to Romeo and Juliet, lovers in William Shakespeare's play of the same name. Chuck was teasing Ray because Beatrice took his hand. He was implying that they, too, were in love.
3. The allusion is to Homer, a poet of ancient Greece. He is credited with writing *The Iliad* and *The Odyssey,* epic poems in which great battles take place. The heroes fight bravely and perform great feats.

Allusions as Context Clues (Page 35)

1. inventor (b)
2. handsome (a)
3. optimist (c)
4. strange (a)
5. detective (b)
6. weak point (a)

Personification: How Human-like! (Pages 38–39)

 1. The sun is personified. It cannot peep into a room, promise, nor see.
 2. The fountain is personified. It can't really play.
 3. Fields and trees are personified. Fields cannot smile, and trees cannot wave.
 4. The sphinx is personified. It can neither smile nor mock.
 5. The mountain is personified. It can neither talk nor predict weather.
 6. The trees are personified by referring to their leaves as clothing.
 7. The road signs are personified. They cannot tease.
 8. Morning is personified. It can neither creep nor be slow.
 9. The house is personified. It cannot crouch.
10. The ebb tide is personified. It cannot be cruel. It can neither make reparation nor deliberately delay.

Anthropomorphism (Page 41)

1. anthropomorphism
2. anthropomorphism
3. personification
4. anthropomorphism
5. personification

Don't Exaggerate! (Page 43)

1. When you are thinking, your wide-open eyes get very large.
2. A shearing had brought a lot of gray wool to be washed and bleached and dyed.
3. When you perspire greatly, there comes a time when you…itch."
4. A while later, we heard the soles of Atticus's shoes scrape the front steps.

Davy Crockett (Page 44)

1. truth
2. exaggeration
3. truth
4. truth
5. exaggeration
6. truth
7. truth
8. exaggeration
9. truth
10. truth

Understatement (Page 46):

Being sucked through a pipe and disappearing is much more than "going on a little journey."

Litote: A Kind of Understatement (Page 48)

"I was not without worry" is the litote. It means that he *was* worried.

Ironic Situations (Page 51)

1. cosmic irony
2. verbal irony
3. dramatic irony
4. verbal irony
5. situational irony

Sarcasm (Page 52)

1. Bear is making fun of Crispin's short answers.
2. Grandma is mocking Mildred. It is obvious that the sheep did not get there on their own.
3. Nadia thinks that time spent with her should be more important than any appointment.

Working with Oxymora (Page 54)

1. "Peaceable war" is the oxymoron. They set up the fence to avoid problems, not to cause them.
2. "Rough kindness" is the oxymoron. Bear was being tough, but he was doing it for Crispin's good.

Figurative Language & Other Literary Devices

Romeo and Juliet (Page 56)
1. The second, fifth, seventh, ninth, and twelfth lines should be circled. The following phrases should be underlined: brawling love, loving hate, heavy lightness, feather of lead, bright smoke, cold fire, sick health, and still-waking sleep.
2. They are in love, but their families hate each other.

Thinking About Symbols (Page 58):
1. The footprint represents Crusoe's mixed feelings about companionship and about rejoining human society. He used to long for these things and now he fears them.
2. The coffee symbolizes Jethro's coming of age. At first he is not given any. When he works in the fields, his brother soaks his bread in it. When he takes on adult responsibilities, he is given it.

Puns (Page 60)
1. It is a play on the word *page,* meaning "a sheet of a book" or "a youth being trained for knight-hood."
2. A Renaissance Man is knowledgeable in several areas. It sounds like Rent-a-Seance Man. Ob was referring to the fact that they were trying to find someone to contact Aunt May, who had died.

Devices of Sound: Alliteration (Page 61)
First example: gruesome, Gilly, gorgeous, gracious, good, glorious, Galadriel, grateful, and grateful. Second example: while, weak, weary; nodded, nearly napping; rapping, rapping; and tapping, 'tis, tapping.

Devices of Sound: Onomatopoeia (Page 62)
These words should be circled: tinkle, tinkle, tinkle, jingling, tinkling, chiming, alarum, clang, clash, roar, twanging, clanging, clamor, clangor, tolling, groan, tolling, tolling, tolling, moaning, and groaning.

Identifying Onomatopoeia (Page 63)
1. whizzing   2. muttered, muttering, grumbling, grumbling, rumbling   3. neigh, squeal

Name The Technique (Pages 68–69)
1. idiom   3. oxymoron   5. pun   7. paradox   9. metaphor   11. litote
2. hyperbole   4. simile   6. litote   8. personification 10. allusion   12. hyperbole

Crossword Puzzle (Page 70)

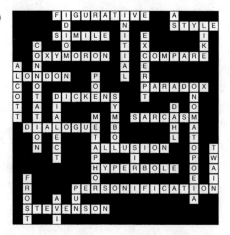

Figurative Language & Other Literary Devices   © Educational Impressions, Inc.

Bibliography & Suggested Reading List

Alcott, Louisa May. *Little Women.* New York: Penguin Group, 2004.

Alexander, Lloyd. *The High King.* New York: Random House, 1969.

Avi. *Crispin.* New York: Hyperion Books, 2002.

Babbitt, Natalie. *Tuck Everlasting.* New York: Farrar, Straus and Giroux, 1985.

Barrie, J.M. *Peter Pan.* New York: Simon & Schuster, 2000.

Burnett, Frances Hodgson. *The Secret Garden.* New York: HarperTrophy, 1998.

Creech, Sharon. *Walk Two Moons.* New York: HarperCollins, 1996.

Curtis, Christopher Paul. *Bud, Not Buddy.* New York: Bantam, Doubleday, Dell, 2002.

Cushman, Karen. *Catherine, Called Birdy.* New York: HarperTrophy, 1995.

——. *The Midwife's Apprentice.* New York: HarperCollins, 1996.

Dahl, Roald. *Charlie and the Chocolate Factory.* New York: Penguin Group, 2002.

——. *James and the Giant Peach.* New York: Penguin Group, 2000.

De Angeli, Marguerite. *A Door in the Wall.* New York: Random House, 1998.

Defoe, Daniel. *Robinson Crusoe.* New York: Aladdin Books, 2001.

Di Camillo, Kate. *The Tale of Despereaux.* Cambridge, Massachusetts: Candlewick, 2006.

Dickens, Charles. *Oliver Twist.* New York: Bantam Books, 1982.

——. *A Tale of Two Cities.* New York: Penguin Group, 2003.

Doyle, Arthur Conan. *The Hound of the Baskervilles.* New York: Aladdin Books, 2000.

——. *The Lost World.* New York: Ballantine Books, 1996.

Forbes, Esther. *Johnny Tremain.* New York: Random House, 1987.

Frost, Robert. *The Poetry of Robert Frost.* New York: Henry Holt & Co., 2002.

Grahame, Kenneth. *The Wind in the Willows.* New York: Aladdin Books, 1989.

Hamilton, Virginia. *The House of Dies Drear.* New York: Aladdin Books, 2006.

Hesse, Karen. *Out of the Dust.* New York: Scholastic, 1997.

Hiaasen, Carl. *Hoot.* New York: Random House, 2006.

Hinton, S.E. *The Outsiders.* New York: Penguin Group, 1997.

Kadohata, Cynthia. *Kira, Kira.* New York: Atheneum, 2004.

Lee, Harper. *To Kill a Mockingbird.* New York: Warner Books, 1987.

London, Jack. *The Call of the Wild.* New York: Aladdin Books, 2003.

Figurative Language & Other Literary Devices

Montgomery, L.M. *Anne of Greene Gables.* New York: Aladdin Books, 2001.

O'Brien, Robert. *Mrs. Frisby and the Rats of NIMH.* New York: Aladdin Books, 1986.

O'Dell, Scott. *Island of the Blue Dolphins.* New York: Bantam, Doubleday, Dell, 1971.

Park, Linda Sue. *A Single Shard.* New York: Houghton Mifflin Company, 2001.

Paterson, Katherine. *The Great Gilly Hopkins.* New York: HarperCollins, 1987.

——. *The Witch of Blackbird Pond.* New York: Random House, 1972.

Paulsen, Gary. *Hatchet.* New York: Simon & Schuster, 1999.

Peck, Richard. *A Long Way from Chicago.* New York: Penguin Group, 2004.

——. *A Year Down Yonder.* New York: Penguin Group, 2002.

Peck, Robert Newton. *A Day No Pigs Would Die.* New York: Random House, 1994.

Perkins, Lynn Rae. *Criss Cross.* New York: Greenwillow, 2004.

Poe, Edgar Allan. *Complete Stories and Poems of Edgar Allan Poe.* New York: Doubleday, 1984.

Raskin, Ellen. *The Westing Game.* New York: Penguin Group, 2004.

Rylant, Cynthia. *Missing May.* New York: Scholastic, 2004.

Rawls, Wilson. *Where the Red Fern Grows.* New York: Bantam Books, 1997.

Sachar, Louis. *Holes.* New York: Random House, 2001.

Sewell, Anne. *Black Beauty.* New York: Simon & Schuster, 2000.

Shakespeare, William. *Romeo and Juliet.* New York: Simon & Schuster, 2004.

Shelley, Mary. *Frankenstein.* New York: Simon & Schuster, 2004.

Speare, Elizabeth George. *The Sign of the Beaver.* New York: Random House, 1984.

——. *The Witch of Blackbird Pond.* New York: Random House, 1978.

Sperry, Armstrong. *Call It Courage.* New York: Aladdin Books, 1990.

Spinelli, Jerry. *Maniac Magee.* New York: Little, Brown & Co., 1999.

Stevenson, Robert Louis. *Treasure Island.* New York: Aladdin Books, 2000.

Taylor, Mildred D. *Roll of Thunder, Hear My Cry.* New York: Penguin Group, 2004.

Twain, Mark. *A Connecticut Yankee in King Arthur's Court.* New York: Bantam, 1983.

——. *The Adventures of Tom Sawyer.* New York: Aladdin Books, 2001.

Verne, Jules. *Around the World in Eighty Days.* New York: Penguin Group, 2004.

Wells, H.G. *War of the Worlds.* New York: Random House, 2002.

Yates, Elizabeth. *Amos Fortune, Free Man.* New York: Penguin Group, 1989.